Watching Water Birds

by Jim Arnosky

NATIONAL
GEOGRAPHIC
SOCIETY

Washington, D.C.

Library of Congress Cataloging-in-Publication Data

Arnosky, Jim.
Watching water birds / Jim Arnosky.
p.   cm.
Summary: Provides a personal look at various species of fresh- and saltwater birds, including loons and grebes,
mergansers, mallards, wood ducks, Canada geese, gulls, and herons.
ISBN: 0-7922-7073-8 (hardcover)   0-7922-6739-7 (paperback)
1. Water birds —Juvenile literature. 2. Water birds—Identification—Juvenile literature.
[1. Water birds. 2. Birds.] I. Title
QL676.2.A773   0997   598.176—dc21   97-7594

THE WORLD'S LARGEST NONPROFIT scientific and educational organization, the National
Geographic Society was founded in 1888 "for the increase and diffusion of geographic knowledge."
Since then it has supported scientific exploration and spread information to its more than eight million
members worldwide. The National Geographic Society educates and inspires millions every day through
magazines, books, television programs, videos, maps and atlases, research grants, the National Geographic
Bee, teacher workshops, and innovative classroom materials. The Society is supported through membership
dues, charitable gifts, and income from the sale of its educational products. Members receive NATIONAL
GEOGRAPHIC magazine—the Society's official journal—discounts on Society products and other benefits.
For more information about the National Geographic Society, its educational programs and publications,
and ways to support its work, please call 1-800-NGS-LINE (647-5463) or write to the following address:

National Geographic Society
1145 17th Street N.W.
Washington, D.C. 20036-4688
U.S.A.

Visit the Society's Web site:
www.nationalgeographic.com

Front Cover: A male wood duck
Title Page: Blue-winged teal atop a beaver lodge

Printed in the United States of America

To my Father

For whom art was order and logic.

Every line he drew

had reason to be.

Every picture he completed made sense.

Introduction

Water birds include all birds that swim, dive, or wade in water. Some water birds are strictly freshwater species. Others are found only around salt water. And there are those that thrive in both fresh- and saltwater environs.

For this book I have chosen to focus on the water birds I know best—my favorites. You may recognize them. Most of these birds live where you do. Some of what you'll read may surprise you. Birds are full of surprises.

Take time and look closely at my paintings. See how each bird's colors and markings are created by the overlapping of many differently marked and colored feathers. Practice drawing birds by copying mine. There is no better way to learn about bird anatomy than drawing. For many of the birds, I've painted life-size pictures of all or of some portion of their bodies. These portraits will give you a truer sense of what the birds are really like.

Herring gull

Wood duck

Double-crested cormorant

White ibis

White egret

I hope to help you learn to identify these water birds whenever or wherever they occur in your area. But beyond simply identifying them, I hope you will wonder about them, and try to guess what they are doing.

Now, come and watch my favorite water birds with me.

— *Jim Arnosky*
Crinkle Cove 1997

Yellowlegs

Loons and Grebes

Loons and grebes are birds you rarely see out of water. Both are diving birds with legs set so far back on the body, for propulsion underwater, that they are quite clumsy on land.

Look for loons on large freshwater lakes or salt bays where the birds have plenty of room for their long, laborious takeoffs. Loons flying over prospective fishing waters know how much space they need and will not land on water bodies too small to take off from.

Grebes are not so specialized. They can be found in any water, fresh or salt, big or small. However, grebes are most often seen in marshy pools, small ponds, and shallow, slow-moving streams. They catch fish and will also dive down and root on the bottom for mollusks.

While wading in a tiny pond, I once accidentally stepped on or near a bottom-feeding pied-billed grebe. The startled bird shot up through the surface and flew away, squawking loudly.

A loon can dive down to depths of 200 feet and easily outswim a trout.

When out of each other's sight, loon mates stay in touch by calling loudly. Male and female loons look alike.

Afloat, two-thirds of a loon's heavy body is underwater.

The so-called common loon is actually an endangered species.

In grebes, both sexes look alike.

The most common grebe—the pied-billed grebe—is named for the black ring around its bill.

The western grebe is the largest grebe in North America and has a long swanlike neck.

There is no chance of anyone stepping on a diving loon. Loons keep their distance from people and stay out in the deepest, coldest waters where they find their favorite food—trout.

Because we only see loons far off in the distance, it is hard to really appreciate their size, which is formidable. Here is a loon shown actual size, swallowing a nine-inch rainbow trout.

Mergansers

Mergansers are diving ducks. Like all diving birds, their legs are set back on the body for underwater kicking. However, merganser legs are not so far back as to make them clumsy out of water. Mergansers are often seen resting on pond banks or standing on river rocks.

In flight, mergansers are streamlined, sharp-winged speedsters. Underwater, mergansers keep their wings tucked in tightly and use their stiff tail feathers to steer. While fishing in our little river, I saw four common mergansers swimming this way, rapidly, in close formation. They swam submerged for many hundreds of feet, rounding the river bend.

Mergansers are sometimes called "sawbills" because of the teethlike, fish-grasping serrations in their long, pointed bills.

Mergansers come in three sizes—small, large, and extra-large.

Hooded merganser   *Red-breasted merganser*   *Common merganser*

Red-breasted merganser—male.(Female is gray with a brown head.)

Common mergansers—male and female. These large birds catch fish up to 15 inches long.

Swimming underwater in formation.

Mergansers can be found in woodland ponds, small streams, large rivers, lakes, and bays.

Male and female hooded mergansers

Where I live the hooded merganser is the first duck to arrive in spring—as soon as there are patches of open water in the frozen streams. Hooded mergansers are fun to watch. They are so lively—splashing, dunking their bills, and flapping their sharp-edged wings. By moving nearer each time the birds dive, I can get quite close without them noticing me.

All mergansers, males and females, have head crests that raise when the birds are excited, worried, or alarmed and lower when the birds relax or dive. The male hooded merganser's head crest is brilliant white and huge. Fully raised, it can be seen at a great distance. I find hooded mergansers on large rivers by looking for the bright white triangle of the male's raised crest.

Hooded mergansers are small, but this doesn't stop them from catching rather large fish. Watching one of these ducks emerge with a fat, five- or six-inch fish is a comical sight. The struggling fish jerks the merganser's head all around. But I've never seen a fish jerk free. The merganser's serrated bill clamps tight and can firmly hold slippery fish.

Male hooded mergansers
shown life-size with crest
fully raised above water,
and compressed during a dive.

Mallards

A mallard "tipping up"

Black ducks, pintails, shovelers, gadwalls, and teal are also surface-feeding ducks that have to tip up to feed underwater.

Mallard ducks are large, hearty ducks that seem to be able to live anywhere. They are the ducks of city parks and farm ponds. I've fished in mountain brooks with mallards quacking upstream. Mallards thrive in freshwater, brackish water (mixed salt and fresh), and salt water. You can find mallards in marshes, swamps, bogs, and even in temporary puddles on fields and lawns after a heavy rain.

Mallards are surface feeders. They are too buoyant to dive and their legs, set midway on the body, are not designed for powerful underwater kicking. To feed below the water surface, mallards must "tip up" and dip their front half under. In this way they feed on aquatic insects, small mollusks, and underwater plants. On land, mallards eat acorns, seeds, grain, and bread crumbs when they are offered.

Watch a mother mallard with her brood. When she shepherds them from behind, she is worried about their safety. When she is out front leading them, she feels entirely safe.

Male mallard

Female mallard

Mallards spend as much
time on land as they
do on water.

Where Do The Wings Go?

Water birds often flap or spread their wings momentarily to stretch a muscle or quickly use their bill to nudge an out-of-place feather back into position. Have you ever wondered where a bird's wings go when the bird is not spreading them? The next time you see a flying bird land, keep your eyes on the way it folds its wings.

1   2   3

In just a few seconds, a bird's broadly spread wings fold closed and tuck completely away under the feathers of the bird's back. That's where wings go!

Female mallard folding and tucking away her wings.

4   5   6

Male wood duck

Wood Duck

Whenever you see a flock of mallards, look at each bird individually. You may find a wood duck or two mingled in the group. That's how I saw my very first wood duck. One afternoon, I had my camera lens focused on some swimming mallards, when suddenly a male wood duck swam into view. It was the most stunningly beautiful bird I'd ever seen. I slowly turned the lens' focus ring until the wood duck's red-orange eye and deep-red eye ring looked clear and sharp. The bird's multicolored bill stood out brilliantly against the background of muddy brown water. The wood duck lingered in that spot a long while. I soaked in every detail.

Ever since that day, the wood duck has been my favorite bird. I've painted many pictures of the spectacular males as well as the lovely gray-brown females. But none of my paintings even came close to the awesome beauty of the actual birds. Until now. The life-size painting you see here, done in acrylics, watercolors, and colored pencils, comes close. If you haven't yet seen your first wood duck, keep looking. When you do, you are in for one of the great thrills of wildlife watching!

Duck or goose?
Which was it?

Duck wings
flap so fast,
they always
look blurred.

You can always see
a goose's wings clearly,
even when they are
flapping

Canada Geese

My wife Deanna can hear geese honking in the sky even while we are driving in the noisy Jeep with all the windows closed. She thrills to the sound. Canada geese are her favorites. Every autumn we visit Dead Creek on the shore of Lake Champlain to see the geese arriving from the north. Dead Creek is one of many stopovers on their migration south for the winter. At Dead Creek there are ponds and marshlands, and most important, grainfields where the geese find sustenance.

When Deanna and I see the multitudes of geese feeding in the fields around Dead Creek, all honking, flapping their wings, and enlivening the air in flight, we know countless more wild geese are doing the same in similar refuges all along the great migration flyways.

Geese mate for life. You can tell which geese in a flock are mates. They stay noticeably close and are attentive to one another. A small group of geese is called a gaggle. Gaggles are often made up of young geese—grown goslings—from the same brood.

A pair of Canada geese

A gaggle of geese

A multitude of geese—many different flocks combined, Canada and snow geese mingling—is a sight to behold! Watch the noisy congregation. Lose yourself in the crowd.

Gulls

Not too many years ago, gulls were strictly coastal birds. You had to go to the seashore to see them. In fact, we called them seagulls. Today many species of gulls can be found far inland, along rivers and around big freshwater lakes. Gulls are the easiest birds to keep in view and in focus with binoculars. They move so slowly and deliberately. In flight, gulls sometimes move so slowly that they appear to be making no headway at all. When a gull flies this slowly over water, it is looking for dead or wounded fish floating on the surface. The instant a fish is spotted, the gull drops to the water and snaps up the morsel in its bill.

All gulls under two years old are mottled gray or brown. Because of this, it is difficult to identify immature gulls according to species. Even as adults, many species of gulls are so similar that you have to look for slight differences in markings. Gulls are often confused with terns. Terns are smaller than gulls. They have swallowlike wings and tails and most have black caps.

Gull wings are angled upward
to keep them high and dry when
a gull dips close to the water for food.

Herring gull

Laughing gull

Ring-billed gull

Immature
ring-billed gull

Common tern

Gulls can swim but they cannot dive. When you see gulls out on the water keeping to the same general area, it is a sign that fish, big ones and small ones, are directly below and a slaughter is underway.

Down below the floating gulls, large predatory fish are feeding on a school of smaller fish. The big fish dog their prey from beneath, waiting for the right moment to rush up and slash through the school. Each time the big fish rush the school, many panicked fish are caught and eaten. Some are attacked yet escape and survive.

Others get away but are severely wounded and float helplessly to the surface, where the waiting gulls snatch them up.

How do gulls locate the schools of fish? Small terrified fish fleeing underwater predators dash away haphazardly, turning broadside to the sunlight. Gulls flying over the water can see through the surface and spot the sparkling sides of fleeing fish.

Herons

A heron can change
its shape drastically
by simply contracting,
or looping in, its neck.

In flight, herons hold
their necks tightly coiled.

Of all the water birds, herons are the most fun to watch. There is a great deal of suspense in their movements as they wade in shallow water—long legs stepping oh-so-slowly; neck stretched and arching forward; eyes unblinking; sharp bill pointed down, ready to spear a fish, tadpole, or frog.

Heron eyes are naturally angled downward, so the birds can always be watching the water. When you think a heron is looking forward, it may actually be intently watching its own footsteps.

In places where egrets are found along with herons, the two can be easily confused. To my eye, heron and egret anatomies are identical. Here's how I identify egrets. If the bird has coal-black legs and feet, it is a great egret. If it has black legs and yellow feet, it is a snowy egret. If it is standing on a cow or a horse, it is a cattle egret.

Just before landing,
a heron will stretch
and lower its neck.

Great blue heron

Green heron

Little blue heron

Night herons are most
often seen silhouetted
against twilight waters.

Herons are watchful and wary birds. It is difficult to sneak close to a heron without spooking it. I like to have something large—a tree or a clump of cattails—between me and the bird. Then, by moving heron-like myself, I can get close enough to watch and even photograph these marvelous creatures.

Every evening at the lake, I look forward to seeing our resident pair of great blue herons coming home to roost. I wonder where they have been all day, what new fishing spots they have found. And as the birds swoop low to land behind the cattails, I think of my own day out on the water, surrounded by the wonderful water birds that beautify our world.

Life-size great blue heron
and leopard frog

JIM ARNOSKY is one of today's leading naturalists writing and illustrating for children. Winner of the Washington Post/Children's Book Guild Award for his overall contribution to nonfiction for children, he has also received the Eva L. Gordon Award for outstanding children's science literature, and the Christopher Award for *Drawing from Nature*, an ALA Notable Book.

He has been called "an inspired teacher" by Roger Tory Peterson, and ALA *Booklist* has said, "It's easy to appreciate nature under this artist's guiding hand."

Jim Arnosky and his wife, Deanna, live in a farmhouse in Northern Vermont that's surrounded by woods with many nearby brooks, streams, ponds, and lakes. The author can often be found in or near or on water, as he is an avid trout fisherman and boatman, and, always, a wildlife watcher.